Original title:
The Puzzle of Pensive Hearts

Copyright © 2024 Creative Arts Management OÜ
All rights reserved.

Author: Cameron Blair
ISBN HARDBACK: 978-9916-90-798-6
ISBN PAPERBACK: 978-9916-90-799-3

The Riddles We Hide Within

In shadows deep where secrets lay,
The heart conceals what words can't say.
Each thought a puzzle, wrapped in fear,
A silent whisper, barely clear.

We wear our masks like fragile glass,
Reflecting truths that slowly pass.
In crowded rooms, we stand alone,
Yet crave the warmth we have not known.

With every smile, a tale unfolds,
A world unseen behind the bold.
We dance on edges, brave and thin,
As riddles twist where dreams begin.

So let us speak in gentle rhyme,
Unlock the stories lost in time.
For in the silence, voices blend,
And riddles wait for hearts to mend.

Lost Keys to Hidden Chambers

In whispers of the quiet night,
A rusted key unlocks with fright.
Forgotten doors from days of old,
Holding secrets yet untold.

Dusty halls and shadows' sweep,
Memories that time does keep.
With every turn, a story reveals,
The hidden truths that time conceals.

Reflections in a Shimmering Pool

Beneath the surface, dreams collide,
In waters deep, where thoughts reside.
Each ripple speaks of hopes once bright,
Captured echoes in soft twilight.

A gaze cast down, serenity found,
In gentle waves that swirl around.
The past flows through like silken thread,
While visions dance in shades of red.

Flickers of Hope in Solitary Dreams

In shadows deep, where fears take flight,
A single spark ignites the night.
Dreams of solace beckon near,
Whispers of courage calm the fear.

Each flicker flares with promise bold,
A story waiting to unfold.
In solitude, the heart will bloom,
Illuminating paths from gloom.

Entangled in Timeless Affection

In every glance, a tale unfolds,
Of hearts entwined, the love that holds.
Moments captured, fleeting, sweet,
A dance of souls, a rhythmic beat.

Beyond the hours, beyond the years,
A bond remains that calms our fears.
Timeless whispers, soft and clear,
An echo of love always near.

Increasingly Uneasy Reflections

In the mirror's gaze, shadows dance,
Each thought a whisper, lost in chance.
Waves of doubt crash on the shore,
Echoes calling, wanting more.

A heart in turmoil, restless and sore,
Seeking calm, yet longing for war.
Fractured dreams on silent nights,
Fleeing thoughts, dimming lights.

Lingering Melodies of Solitude

Notes float softly in the air,
Each harmony a silent prayer.
Strings of time gently unwind,
Moments shared in the mind.

Alone with rhythms that softly play,
Echoes of night merge with the day.
In this space, the heart can feel,
A warmth of comfort, tender and real.

Dance of the Hesitant Hearts

Two souls sway in doubt's embrace,
Uncertain steps in a fragile space.
Eyes that linger, hands that shy,
Yearning hearts that dare not fly.

A shuffle here, a pause to breathe,
Moments linger, hopes we weave.
In every glance, a story starts,
A silent dance of hesitant hearts.

Barriers of the Untold Heart

Walls built high, secrets confined,
Words unspoken, love entwined.
Behind the gates, emotions swell,
In silence, a thousand tales to tell.

Fingers trace the dreams that fade,
In the shadows, promises made.
Hushed desires in starlit nights,
Longing for the softest lights.

Unraveling the Tapestry of Emotion

Threads of joy weave through the pain,
Colors of laughter blend with rain.
Each stitch a secret, each knot a fear,
Unraveling tales we hold dear.

Fingers trace patterns, lost in time,
Echoes of moments, both bitter and prime.
A heart in turmoil, yet beautifully worn,
In this woven silence, new love is born.

Labyrinth of Unspoken Desires

Winding paths concealed by night,
Desires whisper just out of sight.
Each turn a promise, each shadow a sigh,
In this maze of longing, we yearn to fly.

Footsteps falter where dreams entwine,
Hidden chambers where our hearts align.
Yet silence lingers, a heavy mist,
In the labyrinth's heart, we dare not risk.

Shadows Danced with Forgotten Whispers

In twilight's grasp, shadows twirl,
Dances of memories, a faint unfurl.
Forgotten whispers serenade the dark,
Words unsaid, each a subtle mark.

Ghosts of laughter echo in gloom,
Flickering softly, illuminating the room.
In the stillness, the shadows sway,
Tales long buried find light of day.

Heartbeats in a Maze of Memories

Heartbeats echo within the halls,
A symphony where silence calls.
Memories woven like vines of old,
Tales of warmth, of love retold.

Each corner turned, a face reappears,
Echoes of laughter, whispers of tears.
In this maze, we search for the light,
Holding each heartbeat, both tender and bright.

Portraits of Hope and Regret

In the light of dawn's embrace,
Dreams are painted on the sky.
Regrets linger in quiet space,
Yet hope dares to still fly.

Shadows of the past unfold,
Whispered tales on winds that sigh.
In every heart, a story told,
Of yearning souls that dare to try.

Colors fade as time moves on,
Yet vibrant hues refuse to die.
In the silence of a song,
Hope blooms, where sorrows lie.

In every tear, a seed is sown,
Where light and darkness intertwine.
With each breath, we're not alone,
For hope and regret both align.

The Interlude of Lost Connections

In the echoes of a faded call,
Voices linger, then drift away.
Once we stood, now we fall,
Like leaves that dance in the gray.

Memories haunt, like shadows cast,
Moments frozen, time unkind.
Connections lost, forever past,
Yet in the heart, they're intertwined.

Across the miles, the silence grows,
Words unspoken, left to rust.
Yearning for the warmth we chose,
To cherish love, we dare to trust.

In every heartbeat, a silent plea,
To bridge the gaps that fate creates.
For in the loss, we hope to see,
That love endures, and never waits.

Labors of Heart and Mind

In the garden of our dreams,
We toil beneath the sun's gaze.
Nurturing roots with tender schemes,
Harvesting joy in countless ways.

Thoughts collide like storms at sea,
In the quiet of the night we mend.
Crafting futures, we strive to be,
The architects of what we send.

With every challenge, our wills ignite,
Passion fuels the fire inside.
Balancing heart and mind in flight,
A journey where hope's our guide.

In the symphony of work and grace,
We find our purpose intertwined.
In every struggle, we embrace,
The labors of the heart and mind.

Fleeting Echoes of What Once Was

In the twilight of yesterdays,
Memories whisper on the breeze.
Fleeting echoes in sunlit rays,
Carried forth by autumn leaves.

Time slips through like grains of sand,
Moments cherished, lightly pressed.
What was once, we understand,
Lies in our hearts, forever blessed.

Waves of laughter, shadows dance,
Reflections in the minds we hold.
In every glance, a second chance,
To treasure stories left untold.

In the silence, we find our way,
Through echoes that softly play.
For in the heart, they choose to stay,
Fleeting whispers, come what may.

Cracking Codes of Affectionate Hearts

In whispers soft, our secrets dwell,
Unlocking bonds, you know me well.
With every laugh, a puzzle formed,
In tender hues, our hearts adorned.

Each coded glance, a silent plea,
A language shared, just you and me.
Through trials faced, we forge our way,
In love's embrace, we choose to stay.

Maps to the Uncharted Feelings

Beneath the stars, our paths align,
With every heartbeat, a sign divine.
Through valleys low and mountains high,
We trace the maps where feelings lie.

In shadows thick, discoveries bloom,
Unfolding dreams in the hidden room.
With compass hearts, we navigate,
To find the love that won't abate.

Silent Questions in a Noisy World

Amidst the clamor, I seek your gaze,
In silence speaks the love that stays.
Each furrowed brow, a thought unvoiced,
In quiet moments, we rejoice.

Unwritten words float in the air,
A tender grace, a knowing stare.
In the loud rush, we find a space,
For unspoken truths in warm embrace.

Love's Complex Cartography

With intricate lines, our story's drawn,
In every curve, a love reborn.
Through twists and turns, we carve our fate,
In maps of love, we resonate.

Each landmark marks a memory bright,
Guiding us home through darkest night.
In every heart, an atlas grows,
As love's cartography gently flows.

Threads of Remorse and Reflection

In shadows deep, the heart does sigh,
Memories linger, whispers of why.
Glistening tears on a fragile cheek,
Regrets unfold, truth we dare not speak.

In quiet corners, the echoes bide,
Longing for moments we tried to hide.
The woven paths of choices made,
Leave us in silence, unafraid.

Yet from the past, we glean our strength,
In threads of sorrow, we find our length.
With every stitch, a lesson learned,
In the quiet night, our souls are turned.

So here we dwell, amidst the seams,
Finding solace in our dreams.
Though paths are strewn with shades of gray,
We'll weave a tapestry, come what may.

The Enigma of Tender Yearnings

In twilight hues, desires awake,
Silent wishes, hearts softly ache.
An unspoken bond, a glance concealed,
In the depths of night, our fates revealed.

Whispers of longing, like breezes chase,
Tender yearnings in a hidden place.
Scents of jasmine float through the air,
Each fleeting moment a treasure rare.

Shadows dance beneath the moon's embrace,
With every heartbeat, we find our grace.
In the quiet hush, our souls align,
Unraveled hopes, a love divine.

What mysteries lie in glances shared?
The enigma blooms where hearts have dared.
In this secret garden of pure delight,
We lose ourselves in the velvet night.

Fractured Melodies of Affection

In broken chords, our songs unfold,
Tales of love, both warm and cold.
A symphony lost in disarray,
Yet in the chaos, we find our way.

Each note a whisper, a chance to mend,
Through fractured tunes, emotions blend.
Harmonies linger in the air,
Echoes of moments we once could share.

When silence falls, the heartstrings play,
In every silence, a word to say.
The melodies rise and gently sway,
Fractured yet beautiful, they find their way.

As we navigate this tangled dance,
In every heartbeat, we take a chance.
For in the gaps, our love does swell,
Fractured melodies weave a spell.

Secrets Beneath the Starlit Veil

Beneath the stars, secrets unfold,
In whispered hues of dusk, they're told.
A tapestry woven with care and grace,
In the night's embrace, we find our place.

Shadows entwined in soft moonlight,
The heart's confessions, hidden from sight.
Silent promises in darkened skies,
Dreams take flight, where our spirit flies.

Each twinkle hides a yearning heart,
In the cosmos, we play our part.
Under this veil, we dare to share,
The secrets of love, a timeless affair.

In the starlit glow, we laugh and weep,
Holding close what the night will keep.
For beneath this sky, so vast and deep,
Wonders awaken, and souls will leap.

Heartstrings in Dissonance

In shadows where we used to play,
The music fades, it slips away.
Each note a memory, bittersweet,
A haunting echo in my heartbeat.

Your laughter lingers in the air,
Yet silence wraps me in despair.
What once was harmony now breaks,
A fractured song that sorrow makes.

The melodies we built have turned,
In every corner, love is burned.
Our heartstrings frayed, the tension high,
A symphony of silent sighs.

But still I search for notes of light,
To drown the shadows, spark the night.
In dissonance, I'll find my way,
To weave a brighter yesterday.

Whispers Beneath the Surface

Beneath the stillness lies a song,
Where whispered secrets drift along.
They pulse like currents in the deep,
Awake when twilight starts to creep.

The moonlight spills on water's edge,
A silent pact, a solemn pledge.
To dive below the world we know,
And listen close, let go the flow.

In echoes soft, the truths arise,
They swirl like shadows in the skies.
Each whisper holds a tale untold,
Of dreams and fears, both young and old.

I find you in those fleeting sounds,
Where love and longing intertwines.
In depths of night, we come alive,
And in those whispers, we survive.

Echoes from the Abyss of Thought

In corridors of mind I roam,
Through hallways dark, I seek a home.
The echoes haunt with every turn,
In silence, restless shadows yearn.

The weight of thoughts, they press like stone,
A heavy heart, forever alone.
Yet in this void, I hear a call,
To rise above, to break the fall.

With every breath, the chains I break,
To cast aside the fears I make.
From depths of doubt, a spark ignites,
I find my strength in darkest nights.

And as the echoes start to fade,
New paths emerge, I am remade.
In the abyss, I found my truth,
A light within my lost youth.

Dappled Memories of Tenderness

In sunlit glades where shadows dance,
Our laughter weaved through every chance.
The dappled light, a gentle kiss,
A moment wrapped in fragile bliss.

The whispers of the leaves above,
Embrace the warmth of childlike love.
Each memory a petal's fall,
A fragrance sweet, we recall it all.

We painted dreams on canvas wide,
With colors bright, our hearts allied.
In every brushstroke, stories spun,
Together under the golden sun.

Those tender moments linger still,
Eternal echoes, soft and shrill.
In dappled light, we linger near,
For every memory we hold dear.

Captured by Fleeting Moments

Moments slip like grains of sand,
Fleeting whispers, barely planned.
Laughter echoes on the breeze,
Time dances with such gentle ease.

Each sunset paints a story bright,
Fading softly into night.
The clock hands spin, a swift embrace,
Memories linger, a warm trace.

In a blink, they come and go,
Chasing shadows, stealing slow.
Yet in our hearts they find their place,
Captured minutes, a blissful chase.

The Conundrum of Silent Sighs

Beneath the surface, whispers hide,
Secrets linger, hearts collide.
A silent breath, a fleeting glance,
In muted words, we find our chance.

Eyes that speak, yet lips stay sealed,
In quiet moments, truths revealed.
What lies beneath the calm facade?
A tangled web, a fragile nod.

With every sigh, a world unfolds,
In silence bold, a tale retold.
The conundrum, a dance of souls,
Within the silence, love consoles.

Intricate Patterns of Unseen Love

In the shadows, whispers thread,
Patterns woven, softly spread.
A glance exchanged, a fleeting touch,
Intricate designs, meaning much.

Hearts entwined in secret grace,
Unseen love, a warm embrace.
Moments bloom like flowers rare,
In gentle folds, we find our care.

In every heartbeat, stories rise,
An exquisite dance, beneath the skies.
Though hidden paths may seem uncharted,
In unseen love, we are unparted.

Heartstrings Tied in Twisted Knots

Heartstrings pull in every space,
Tangled ties, a soft embrace.
With every tug, emotions sway,
In complicated hues, they play.

Knots of joy, knots of pain,
In this tapestry, we remain.
A thread of hope, a clasp of fear,
Each woven moment brings us near.

Yet in the jumbles, love holds tight,
In twisted paths, we find our light.
Through every twist that life bestows,
Our heartstrings sing, and boldly grow.

Conundrums of Connection

In the silence of a crowded room,
Eyes meet, yet words elude their bloom.
A smile flickers, a spark ignites,
What lies beneath these shared sights?

Thoughts entwined like ivy's grip,
Secrets whisper with each heartbeat's trip.
Closeness felt yet distance remains,
A puzzle scattered on the plains.

Feelings dance like shadows at dusk,
Yearning held tight, yet still we distrust.
Echoes linger in uncharted air,
What binds us close, or leads to despair?

Together apart, a curious plight,
In the warmth of day but lost at night.
Each thread we weave, a tangled thread,
In the fabric of being, much left unsaid.

Enigmas Wrapped in Time

Moments flicker like candlelight,
Shadows cast in fading sight.
A clock ticks softly in the room,
Binding past and future's loom.

Whispers of ages lost and found,
Each tick a story, profound.
Pages turn in the book of days,
In silent echoes, memory plays.

Every second a question asked,
As we wear our masks, unmasked.
Time's embrace, both gentle and fierce,
With every layer, our hearts it pierce.

Yet in the dance, a rhythm flows,
Through time's embrace, love still grows.
Enigmas wrapped in moments rare,
A timeless tale we learn to share.

Reflections Through a Glass Heart

A fragile heart encased in glass,
Holds reflections of moments past.
Each glance through its shimmering coat,
Sings of love's sweet, silent note.

Cracks that mar the perfect view,
Tell of heartache and joys anew.
In shards collide both light and dark,
A mosaic bright with every spark.

Yet still it beats with fervent grace,
Finding beauty in every trace.
Through glassy stoicism we yearn,
For honest truth, our hearts to learn.

In the light, the reflections flow,
Through the glass, emotions grow.
Fragile yet strong, a dance of art,
In the realm of love, a glass heart.

Love's Intricate Dialogues

Words woven in a delicate thread,
Whispered secrets softly said.
Each tone a brushstroke, painting trust,
In the canvas of a bond robust.

Arguments dance in playful jest,
Hearts collide, but still find rest.
Emotions rise like tides at sea,
In discourse deep, we learn to be.

Silence speaks in gentle hues,
In knowing glances, we find clues.
Layers peel back, truth laid bare,
A conversation rich, beyond compare.

In every laugh, in every sigh,
Love speaks boldly, never shy.
In intricate patterns, hearts entwine,
In this dialogue, forever divine.

Winding Roads of Emotional Navigation

Through twisting paths of thought we tread,
Where shadows linger, torn and spread.
Each turn a choice, a dismal chance,
To lose ourselves in life's vast dance.

The compass spins, its truth unsure,
In depths of doubt, we seek a cure.
With every step, the heart will guide,
Through winding roads, where dreams reside.

Hope glimmers faint, a distant star,
Yet drives us forth, no matter how far.
In storms of fear, we find our way,
Navigating night, to greet the day.

The journey forms our very core,
Through ups and downs, we learn to soar.
In every curve, our spirit grows,
A testament to where love flows.

Ephemeral Glimpses of What Was

Fleeting moments, soft and bright,
Captured shadows in fading light.
Memories dance, a ghostly waltz,
Echoes whisper of past exalts.

Fragments linger like soft sighs,
A tapestry of laughs and cries.
In stillness hums a tender tune,
Of yesterdays beneath the moon.

Time slips through like grains of sand,
Slipping softly from our hand.
Yet in the heart, they find a place,
Ephemeral glimpses we still embrace.

As seasons turn and pages flip,
The taste of joy in every sip.
Though shadows fade, the love remains,
In every heartbeat, still it reigns.

Heart's Whisper Among the Clamor

In bustling streets, where voices roar,
A quiet pulse beneath the floor.
The heart it whispers, soft and low,
Amidst the chaos, love will flow.

Each clamor fades when feelings swell,
In secrets shared, we break the spell.
Through crowded rooms, a glance, a beat,
In silent moments, worlds compete.

Yet in that noise, we forge our path,
Resilient souls amid the wrath.
The heart's soft murmur guides us true,
To find the light in shades of blue.

Listen close, for therein lives,
The pulse that breathes, that quietly gives.
Among the clamor, a gentle sigh,
A love that blooms, that dares to fly.

Patterns of a Fragile Heart

In delicate threads, emotions weave,
Patterns form, in shades we believe.
Each stitch a story, layered deep,
A tapestry where sorrows sleep.

Fragile forms, yet strong they stand,
Bridges built with trembling hand.
Hearts dance lightly, through joy and pain,
In patterns forged from love's domain.

Like petals falling, soft and bare,
Each moment cherished, stripped of care.
In every crack, potential glows,
A fragile heart, but courage flows.

Through shifting tides and tempests wild,
We learn to love, the heart a child.
In every pattern, truth imparts,
The beauty held in fragile hearts.

Layers of Love's Complexity

Like petals of a rose in bloom,
Each layer hides a different tune.
Whispers soft, secrets deep,
In every heart, a promise to keep.

The light and shadow gently play,
In twilight's glow, emotions sway.
Beneath the surface, stories lie,
A tapestry of laugh and sigh.

With each caress, new textures found,
In tangled threads, we are unbound.
A dance of souls, a quest divine,
In love's embrace, our stars align.

Through storms and calm, we navigate,
The seas of trust, a fragile state.
Yet still we find a way to see,
The beauty in love's complexity.

Heartfelt Whims in Wanderlust

With maps unfurled and dreams in tow,
We chase the sun where wild winds blow.
Each step a rhythm, a beat to find,
In every heartbeat, adventure entwined.

Starlit nights call out our names,
Through valleys deep and mountain flames.
The world unfolds like a storybook,
In whispered tales, we take a look.

Dancing shadows, fleeting sights,
In search of joy on endless nights.
With open hearts and laughter's sound,
In every moment, love is found.

Through distant shores and twilight skies,
Each journey penned with endless tries.
In wanderlust, together we roam,
Our hearts forever find their home.

Faded Memories in Soft Hues

In soft hues, the past appears,
Fleeting whispers of our years.
A photograph in sepia tones,
Where laughter echoes, and love roams.

Time drips slowly like melting glass,
Moments suspended as they pass.
Each shade a story, tender and true,
In faded dreams, I find you anew.

The corners of my mind reside,
In gentle shades where feelings hide.
With every glance, old tales revive,
In colored memories, we still thrive.

Though time may blur what once was bright,
In soft hues, we find the light.
Wrapped in the warmth of memories dear,
Our faded love will persevere.

Refractions of a Tender Spirit

A prism cast in soft embrace,
Reflects a world of boundless grace.
From gentle hands and glowing hearts,
A tender spirit that never departs.

In laughter bright and quiet tears,
We weave our dreams, dissolve our fears.
Through every challenge, trust remains,
In love's reflection, joy sustains.

The colors dance in morning light,
Each shimmer speaks of timeless flight.
With every breath, we spark anew,
In sacred moments, me and you.

Let kindness flow like rivers wide,
In tender spirits, love will guide.
Through every storm and sunlit dawn,
In unity, our hearts respond.

Lattice of Unresolved Desires

In the stillness, whispers call,
Threads of dreams begin to sprawl.
Fingers trace the air's facade,
Hopes entwined with every nod.

Hidden wishes dance in light,
Bob and weave, take flight at night.
Hearts on strings, they twist and sway,
In the lattice, lost, they play.

Shattered pieces, glimmers rare,
Unraveled care, a silent stare.
Yearnings captured, soft and bright,
In the lattice, love ignites.

Yet the shadows softly creep,
Guarding secrets we all keep.
In the weave of night we roam,
A labyrinth, we're far from home.

Chasing Shadows of the Heart

Fleeting echoes in the night,
Yearning whispers take their flight.
In the corners, shadows play,
Dancing dreams in disarray.

Through the alleys of the mind,
Lost in sweetness, hard to find.
Every heartbeat drips with doubt,
Chasing whispers, scream and shout.

Fingers grasp at what is near,
Each soft murmur, lost in fear.
Heartbeats sync with fading light,
Chasing shadows, holding tight.

Yet in twilight's tender glow,
Love will linger, ebb and flow.
In the distance, hope will gleam,
Fading shadows, waking dream.

Portraits of Melancholy

Each stroke whispers tales untold,
Portraying hearts both brave and bold.
Colors fade, soft and gray,
In the silence, shadows play.

Gazes locked in painted bliss,
Hints of longing, deep abyss.
Every canvas bleeds the pain,
Melancholy's sweet refrain.

With every layer, secrets bloom,
Hanging still in quiet room.
Brushes dance with tender care,
Lifetimes captured, thin air.

Yet the beauty drips with tears,
Memories crafted through the years.
In each portrait, love resides,
Melancholy, where hope abides.

Interwoven Paths of Affection

In the garden, roots entwine,
Hearts now flourish, softly shine.
Paths once tangled, now aligned,
In the weave, true love defined.

Every step brings forth a song,
Guiding notes where we belong.
Hands in hands, we dance and flow,
In this rhythm, hearts will grow.

Moments stitched with vibrant thread,
Spun together, feared and fed.
Through the trials, bonds set tight,
Interwoven, pure delight.

Yet the journeys, sometimes steep,
Carrying dreams we long to keep.
In the tapestry, paths conjoin,
In affection, we find our point.

Shades of Unresolved Longing

In shadows deep where silence reigns,
A whisper calls, a ghost remains.
With every sigh, the night unfolds,
A tale of love, yet untold.

Moonlight dances on distant dreams,
Stirring hope amid the screams.
Yet hands that grasp the empty air,
Find only echoes of despair.

The heart, it yearns for something more,
A fleeting glimpse, a passing door.
Yet time drifts by, a restless tide,
As longing's depth we cannot hide.

Beneath the surface, questions stir,
In every pause, in every blur.
For in the dark, the truth resides,
In shades of love, where pain abides.

Interludes of a Dreamer's Heart

Softly spinning thoughts of grace,
In starlit realms, I find my place.
Where wishes blend with moonlit sighs,
And every star sparks endless cries.

A canvas stretched, my heart displayed,
In colors bright, the small charade.
Each fleeting glance, a brush of fate,
In gentle strokes, the dreams await.

Through corridors of time I roam,
In echoes sweet, I feel at home.
With every heartbeat, every chance,
I lose myself within the dance.

Yet shadows linger, doubts appear,
A fleeting thought, a quivering tear.
Still in my dreams, I chase the light,
In interludes that spark the night.

Curious Currents of Emotion

Waves that crash against the shore,
Each ebb and flow, I crave for more.
The tide of hope, a gentle push,
Pulls me forward, into the hush.

In every tear, a story flows,
From hidden depths, the heart bestows.
A mixture sweet of joy and pain,
In fleeting moments, love remains.

Curious hearts like rivers run,
Chasing dreams beneath the sun.
With every turn, a lesson learned,
In currents wild, my spirit burned.

Yet still I seek the quiet stream,
Where peace resides and soft winds dream.
Among the chaos, find the calm,
In curious waves, I write my psalm.

Echoes Through the Heart's Chamber

In chambers vast, the echoes ring,
With every beat, the memories cling.
A symphony of love and loss,
In whispered tones, I bear the cross.

Through corridors of time I tread,
Haunting whispers of words unsaid.
Each fragment held, a piece of me,
In shadows cast, I yearn to be.

The heart, a vault of hopes and fears,
Resounding laughter, mingled tears.
Within these walls, the past persists,
In echoes' grace, the heart insists.

Yet through the dark, a light will break,
Illuminating paths we take.
For in these echoes, I find the way,
Through heart's chamber, to a new day.

Secrets Carved in Soft Shadows

In twilight's grasp, whispers blend,
Secrets linger, time won't mend.
Flickering light through leafy shade,
In silence, hidden truths cascade.

Each shadow tells a tale untold,
In patterns soft, the night is bold.
Hearts entwined in a gentle dance,
A moment seized, a fleeting glance.

Moonlit paths where dreams decay,
Lost in echoes, fade away.
Carved in dusk, the secrets wade,
In memories where hopes are laid.

Yet in the dark, a spark ignites,
Fueling the fire of starry nights.
Soft shadows guard what must remain,
In the quiet, love's sweet refrain.

Threads of Complicated Affection

Tangled hearts in a woven mess,
Each thread speaks of love's excess.
In hues of joy, in shades of pain,
We dance through storms, we learn to feign.

Bound by fate, yet yearning free,
Entangled souls, a mystery.
In laughter's sound, in sorrow's weight,
We navigate this twisted fate.

Fragile ties in a world so grand,
We grasp at dreams just out of hand.
Through winding paths, our stories flow,
In streams of laughter, tears will show.

Yet in each stitch, a bond defined,
Complicated, yet intertwined.
In every heartbeat, a truth revealed,
Love's fabric holds, though sometimes concealed.

Heartbeats in a Distant Fog

Through the mist, faint pulses rise,
Heartbeats echo, soft lullabies.
In the stillness, whispers call,
Through the haze, I feel it all.

Each moment lost, yet held so near,
In shadows whispered, I can hear.
A distant drum in twilight's hold,
A symphony of stories told.

Neon nights wrapped in soft grey,
Guided by beats that lead the way.
In the silence, a yearning grows,
As the heartbeat of night softly flows.

In the fog, we drift and sway,
Finding solace where dreams play.
Every thrum a promise kept,
In the fog, our secrets slept.

Labyrinths of Lingering Looks

In a glance, a world unspun,
Labyrinth paths where two are one.
Eyes collide, a spark ignites,
In silent realms of starry nights.

Twisted paths, they weave and bind,
In every look, the heart's designed.
A language shared without a word,
In the silence, feelings stirred.

With every turn, the tension grows,
In myriad ways affection flows.
Through shadowed corners, light will peek,
In the depths, our hearts will speak.

Yet in this maze, we lose our way,
With lingering looks that come to play.
A circle drawn, a dance so true,
In the labyrinth, it's me and you.

The Map to Uncharted Feelings

In a quiet heart, secrets dwell,
Paths unwritten, stories to tell.
An inked compass points the way,
To feelings that dance and sway.

Beneath the stars, emotions bloom,
Like flowers bright in a shadowed room.
With every step, the courage grows,
To navigate through highs and lows.

A treasure chest of dreams unspun,
Where every heartbeat feels like fun.
The map unfolds in tender grace,
Leading me to a warm embrace.

Through valleys deep and mountains high,
I chase the whispers of the sky.
Each mark I make, a journey new,
To uncharted feelings, pure and true.

Reflections on a Shattered Mirror

Fragments glisten, stories told,
In every shard, a memory bold.
I gaze deeper, see my soul,
In the cracks, I find my whole.

Shadows dance on the broken floor,
Echoes linger, forevermore.
Each piece reflects a silent scream,
An artful chaos, a haunting dream.

With gentle touch, I mend the split,
Creating light from darkest wit.
The mirror shows not just despair,
But beauty hidden, if I dare.

In fractured glass, I search and seek,
For strength in moments soft yet bleak.
A reflection whole, though once it tore,
In shattered truths, I find my core.

Whimsy in the Depths of Solitude

In quiet nooks where shadows play,
Imagination finds its way.
The whispers of the midnight breeze,
Bring whimsical thoughts that aim to please.

A lonely dance beneath the stars,
Each twirl a story, soft and Mars.
Colors twist in the darkened lane,
Where solitude sings, free from pain.

With laughter echoing through my mind,
I paint the night, bright and unconfined.
Every moment, a playful song,
In depths of silence, I feel strong.

As dreams take flight on wings of night,
I find my solace in soft delight.
A world alive, though I stand still,
In whimsy's grip, my heart does thrill.

A Canvas of Yearning Shadows

On a blank canvas, colors blend,
Yearning shadows whisper and send.
Each stroke a story, deep and wide,
Of love and loss that cannot hide.

Brushes dance with gentle grace,
Capturing time's soft embrace.
In every hue, a tale unfolds,
Of dreams once bright, now bittersweet gold.

The shadows linger, rich and deep,
In every corner, secrets keep.
A tapestry of heart and pain,
Each layer speaks of joy and strain.

As light filters through the dusky veil,
Hope emerges where shadows prevail.
A canvas waiting for hearts to share,
In every longing, love's soft care.

Whispers of Fragmented Dreams

In the quiet night, shadows play,
Fragments of thoughts drift away,
Whispers caught in the moon's glow,
Leaving trails of what we know.

Silent wishes on the breeze,
Dancing with the swaying trees,
Dreams like leaves in autumn fall,
Echoes of a distant call.

Moments fleeting, time will bend,
To the stories of heart's mend,
Whispers linger, softly sigh,
In the realm where dreams may lie.

Life's reflections, all obscure,
In the dreamscape, we find cure,
Whispers weave with threads of light,
Guiding us through endless night.

Echoes Within the Silent Chamber

Within the walls, shadows reside,
Echoes of laughter, where dreams hide,
Silent whispers beckon near,
Threads of longing, crystal clear.

Memories dance on the floor,
Timeless tales and hearts that soar,
In the chamber, whispers blend,
Carving paths that never end.

Faces fade into the night,
Each one lost, yet holding tight,
In the silence, echoes throng,
Binding hearts with unseen song.

Chambered thoughts in quiet space,
Time can never erase their grace,
Echoes linger, rich and deep,
In our hearts, forever keep.

Pieces of a Heart's Dilemma

Scattered shards in twilight's glow,
Pieces of a heart's soft woe,
Fragments lost, yet wanting whole,
Yearning whispers, silent soul.

Paths diverge in endless night,
Choices made in fading light,
Holding on to what we feel,
Bound by threads that seem unreal.

Caught in dreams of what might be,
Fearing love's fragility,
Every piece tells tales untold,
In the warmth, our hearts unfold.

Searching for the missing part,
In the depths of each lost heart,
Pieces sing a tender tune,
Guiding us toward the moon.

Mosaics of Longing Souls

Mosaics built of broken days,
Longing hearts in soft displays,
Colors scattered, chips of glass,
Each a story, none shall pass.

Fragments shine in the sun's glow,
Whispers of wishes that we sow,
In the art of what we crave,
Boundless dreams that souls can pave.

Every shard, a melody,
Blending notes of harmony,
Creating beauty in the seams,
Weaving life through tender dreams.

Longing dances in the night,
Mosaics born from purest light,
In the space where souls ignite,
Fragments shimmer, hearts take flight.

Stitches of Time-Bound Affection

In the fabric of dreams we sew,
Threads of laughter, whispers low.
Every moment, a careful stitch,
Binding hearts without a hitch.

Memories flicker like fading light,
In every shadow, love's delight.
Time bends softly, a gentle sway,
Holding close what will not stray.

Through the years, we weave a tale,
Sturdy as stone, as light as sail.
Each day a patch, each night a seam,
In cozy warmth, we share our dream.

With hands entwined, we face the flow,
Stitches of time, forever grow.
In this quilt of love we find,
Threads unbroken, hearts aligned.

Navigating the Stream of Sentiment

In the river of thought, we float,
Drifting softly, like a boat.
Waves of feeling, currents strong,
Guiding us where we belong.

Whispers dance upon the tide,
As we search, our hearts collide.
Raindrops weave into the stream,
Together we chase every dream.

At the bends where shadows play,
We find comfort, come what may.
Floating freely, hand in hand,
Navigating this vast land.

Time flows gently, never still,
We ride its rhythm, feel its thrill.
In this journey, love's embrace,
A safe harbor, a sacred space.

Whims of a Wistful Soul

In a garden where wishes bloom,
Softly glows the evening gloom.
Whispers carried on the breeze,
Wistful thoughts that seek to please.

Butterflies dance in twilight's hue,
While shadows fade, hopes renew.
With every sigh, a story told,
Of fleeting dreams and hearts of gold.

Stars ignite the velvet sky,
Echoes of a gentle sigh.
Each moment tastes of sweet regret,
In paths where longing's deeply set.

Caught between what's lost and found,
A wistful heart, in love profound.
In the night, where soft dreams stroll,
Lies the essence of my soul.

Quiet Conversations of Longing

In the silence, whispers rise,
Comfort found in gentle sighs.
Eyes that linger, words unsaid,
In this hush, our spirits wed.

Through the stillness, feelings flow,
In every glance, the truth we know.
Lingering touch, a tender grace,
Mapping love upon our space.

In shadows cast by moonlight bright,
Two souls speak without a fight.
Every heartbeat, a silent plea,
In quietude, just you and me.

Longing weaves through every thread,
In unspoken words, we're led.
In this moment, time stands still,
Quiet conversations hold the thrill.

Still Waters of Reflection

In quiet depths, the shadows play,
Ripples form, then drift away.
Moonlight dances, soft and clear,
Whispers echo, close yet near.

Beneath the surface, secrets wait,
Stories linger, seal their fate.
Each glance a mirror, truth to find,
In stillness, peace, our hearts unwind.

Time flows gently, soft embrace,
In solitude, we find our place.
Clear as crystal, thoughts collide,
In waters deep, we cannot hide.

Still reflections of the soul,
Nature's silence makes us whole.
In tranquil moments, visions gleam,
Awakened hearts, embracing dream.

Hidden Paths of the Heart

Amidst the thorns, a blossom grows,
A gentle touch where longing flows.
Twisting trails where feelings start,
Leading softly, hidden art.

In whispered winds, our secrets share,
Every heartbeat, a silent prayer.
With every step, our spirits lift,
To find the love, the greatest gift.

Veiled in mist, the journey calls,
Through winding roads and ancient walls.
Courage blooms where doubts reside,
In every shadow, love's our guide.

Following footsteps, lost and found,
In tender moments, hearts unbound.
With each embrace, our truths impart,
On these hidden paths of heart.

Fabric of Fleeting Emotions

Threads of laughter, tears entwined,
Woven moments, sweet and blind.
Fleeting whispers, time does steal,
In every heartbeat, love is real.

Colors changing, shades of pain,
Silken threads of joy remain.
Tapestry of moments weave,
In life's embrace, we learn to grieve.

In a blink, a sigh, a glance,
Each fleeting spark ignites a dance.
Fading softly into night,
Yet in our hearts, they burn so bright.

In the fabric, threads of fate,
Emotions linger, never late.
Crafted gently, life's design,
In every stitch, your hand in mine.

Serpentine Roads of Desire

Winding paths like whispered dreams,
Curvy lines and silver streams.
In shadows where our secrets dwell,
Desire's echo, a magic spell.

With every turn, the heart ignites,
Chasing stars on sleepless nights.
Fleeting moments of blissful fire,
Lost in dreams that never tire.

Curves and bends, we drift along,
In the rhythm, we belong.
Traversing through the unknown trails,
On serpentine roads that life entails.

With every mile, the passion grows,
In every heartbeat, love bestows.
Embracing paths where shadows play,
On serpentine roads, we find our way.

Fluctuations of a Restless Spirit

In shadows deep, I find my way,
Through whispering winds, I dare to sway.
Each thought a surge, each breath a pull,
A restless heart, both wild and full.

Beneath the stars, I chase the night,
Fleeting moments, a fading light.
Lost in a dance, where time stands still,
Embracing change, against my will.

The tides of fate, they rise and fall,
With every echo, I hear the call.
In every flicker, a spark ignites,
A journey unknown, through endless nights.

To find my place within this maze,
A restless spirit in constant chase.
Through leaps of faith, I carve my path,
In the arms of chaos, I find my wrath.

Soft Sirens of Memory

Whispers of days gone softly play,
In twilight's glow, where shadows sway.
A gentle voice, a tender sigh,
In every echo, dreams imply.

Fleeting glimpses of laughter shared,
Moments cherished, moments bared.
The softest touch, a warmth held tight,
Like morning dew, in the softest light.

Through faded halls, their songs still ring,
A melody that time can't bring.
In every turn, a hidden glance,
The siren's call, my heart's romance.

With every breath, I weave a thread,
To capture all the words unsaid.
In the web of life, they gently bind,
Soft sirens of memory, intertwined.

Delicate Labors of Love

With gentle hands, we tend the seams,
A patchwork woven from our dreams.
Each stitch a promise, each knot a vow,
In the silent hours, we labor now.

Through whispered hopes and tender care,
We build a world, with love to share.
Like flowers blooming in morning's light,
Delicate labors, a wondrous sight.

In laughter's echo, our spirits soar,
In humble gestures, we find our core.
With every glance, a universe spins,
The delicate dance where true love begins.

In the quiet moments, we find our grace,
In the warm glow of a familiar place.
Through time and trials, our hearts remain,
Delicate labors, a sweetness gained.

Enchanted Echoes of Hushed Dreams

In twilight's hush, where spirits play,
Enchanted echoes drift away.
With whispered tales in the moon's embrace,
Hushed dreams awaken, time can't erase.

The gentle stroke of a painter's brush,
Colors entwined in a silken hush.
Through every sigh, the stars descend,
Enchanted whispers that never end.

In hidden realms, where fantasies gleam,
We find solace in the softest dream.
With every heartbeat, the magic flows,
In enchanted echoes, the wonder grows.

So let us wander where shadows weave,
In the lullaby of dusk, we believe.
Through the night, as the world holds its breath,
Enchanted echoes of life and death.

A Tapestry of Troubled Affections

In shadows deep, our whispers toil,
Bound by fate, yet hearts embroil.
A dance of hope, a thread of pain,
Entangled dreams, in love's refrain.

Through storms we sail, our compass lost,
Torn between passion and the cost.
Fingers clasped, our fears held tight,
A tapestry woven from day to night.

In silence, light fights through the fray,
As troubled hearts find words to say.
Each stitch a memory, woven slow,
In every tear, our spirits grow.

What once was whole now frays apart,
Yet beauty breathes within the heart.
With threads of sorrow, threads of grace,
We mend the fabric, embrace our place.

Silent Soliloquies of the Heart

In quiet rooms, the echoes drift,
Words unspoken, a precious gift.
Between the beats, our secrets lie,
In silent dreams, we learn to fly.

Each glance a story, each sigh a song,
In hidden truths, we both belong.
No need for noise, when souls can speak,
In stillness found, we seek what's deep.

Time stands still, as moments freeze,
A gentle breeze, with whispered ease.
Through tangled paths, our spirits roam,
In tender silence, we find our home.

Beneath the stars, our hearts unfold,
In hushed confessions, love is bold.
The world fades out, just you and I,
In silent soliloquies, we fly.

Unraveled Threads of Emotion

A tapestry torn, colors collide,
Threads once entwined now drift aside.
Heartstrings frayed, in chaos they play,
Unraveled dreams at the dawn of day.

With every touch, a moment slips,
Emotions spill from trembling lips.
Fleeting shadows dance in the haze,
As memories fade in life's cruel maze.

Hope whispers softly, a distant call,
In tangled yarns, we rise, we fall.
Through joy and sorrow, we stitch anew,
Unraveled threads bring forth the true.

The fabric of us, both worn and grand,
In every knot, we find our strand.
From frayed beginnings, love will mend,
Through unraveled threads, our hearts will blend.

Mosaic of Hidden Longings

A canvas bright, yet shades of gray,
Fragmented dreams in bright array.
Each piece a story, longing to show,
In every corner, feelings flow.

With shattered hope, yet beauty blooms,
In whispers soft, we chase our blooms.
Through colored glass, our spirits shine,
Mosaic hearts, a love divine.

Within the gaps, secrets reside,
With every shard, our truths abide.
We dance on edges, brave the night,
In hidden longings, we find our light.

Bound by moments, stitched with care,
In this mosaic, love lays bare.
A puzzle complete, with all its scars,
In unity, we reach for stars.

Harmonies of a Distant Heartbeat

In twilight's glow, whispers arise,
Beneath the stars, where silence lies.
Echoes of love drift in the breeze,
Carrying dreams through swaying trees.

A heartbeat strong, yet far away,
Like shadows dancing at the break of day.
Connections drawn, unseen and tight,
Guided by the soft silver light.

Time holds its breath, a gentle pause,
As nature sings without a cause.
In every pulse, a story spun,
Of harmonies shared, now just begun.

With each soft sigh, a thread is sewn,
In distant hearts, love's seeds are sown.
A melody played from afar,
In silent chords beneath the stars.

The Unfolding of Hidden Truths

Beneath the layers of silent thought,
Lie whispers of what time forgot.
Truths entwined in shadows' embrace,
Yearning to find their rightful place.

With every dawn, new light discerns,
The paths of fate where the soul yearns.
Glimmers of hope in every glance,
As life unveils its secret dance.

Like petals drawn from a fragrant bloom,
Each revelation clears the gloom.
Hidden feelings, tender and bright,
Emerge like stars from the depth of night.

In every heart, a treasure lies,
Guarded by fear, yet bold and wise.
The unfolding waits, a sacred art,
To reveal the truths that dwell in the heart.

Constellations of Silent Affection

In the velvet night, where shadows play,
Constellations blink with love's sway.
Each distant star, a bond so dear,
Whispering tales only hearts can hear.

Silent wishes float on celestial breeze,
With every twinkle, the soul's heart sees.
Moments shared in the hush of time,
Painted in whispers, a sacred rhyme.

Through cosmic dance, our spirits align,
In every heartbeat, your light is mine.
A tapestry woven in twilight's hue,
Constellations' glow reflecting you.

In the stillness, we find our way,
Guided by love's gentle sway.
Together we dream, beneath the skies,
In these constellations, affection lies.

A Dance of Sorrow and Joy

In the quiet corners of our plight,
Sorrow dances with beams of light.
Steps entwined in a tender embrace,
Finding solace in the heart's space.

Tears fall softly like morning dew,
While laughter echoes, pure and true.
In shadows cast by the light above,
A waltz of contrasts, a song of love.

With every heartbeat, joy takes flight,
Crowned by the presence of gentle night.
A ballet unfolds, where emotions meet,
In this intricate rhythm, life is sweet.

Through darkest hours and brightest days,
We learn to dance in myriad ways.
Embodying life, in rhythm and rhyme,
A dance of sorrow and joy through time.

Echoes of a Lost Lament

In the stillness, whispers sigh,
Memories linger, fade and die.
Footsteps chase the paths once known,
In shadows cast, I walk alone.

A gentle breeze through trees does weave,
Carrying tales of love that grieve.
Each echo lingers, bittersweet,
In every heartbeat, I feel defeat.

Stars above, a distant light,
Remind me of our last goodnight.
The moon reflects my silent tear,
In depths of night, I feel you near.

Yet in the dawn, hope takes its flight,
Turning sorrow into light.
From darkened clouds, a sun will rise,
With time, the heart learns to disguise.

Tangles of Thoughtful Yearnings

In quiet corners, dreams unfold,
Whispers of wishes, brave and bold.
Each thought a thread, it's softly spun,
A tapestry of hearts once won.

Through tangled paths where shadows blend,
Yearnings dance, but never mend.
Lost in the labyrinth of the mind,
Searching for what's left behind.

A flicker of hope, a distant star,
Leading my journey, though it's far.
In every longing, a spark ignites,
Illuminating darkened nights.

Yet tangled dreams can find their way,
With every dawn, a new display.
Yearnings weave a strength so deep,
In the heart's embrace, we learn to leap.

Intricacies of Love's Labyrinth

In spiral turns where lovers meet,
Each glance a riddle, bittersweet.
Hand in hand, we weave and spin,
Navigating where love begins.

Passages twist, shadows entwine,
In every heartbeat, your pulse aligns.
A dance of fate, we take our flight,
In the maze of dreams, we find our light.

Every kiss, a secret sign,
A map of souls that intertwine.
Through walls of doubt, we push and shove,
In the intricate chase of love.

Yet in this maze, I feel you near,
Your whispers calm, drown out the fear.
With every turn, our spirits soar,
In love's labyrinth, forevermore.

Shadows of Unvoiced Sentiments

In silent rooms where echoes dwell,
Words unspoken cast their spell.
Thoughts linger heavy, fill the air,
Shadows dance, a tender scare.

Beneath the surface, feelings swell,
In quiet moments, we know so well.
Each glance a book, each sigh a phrase,
Unvoiced truths in twilight's haze.

As stars blink down, our hearts collide,
In uncharted realms where dreams reside.
Amidst the silence, I feel your soul,
In shadows deep, we become whole.

Yet still, those words hide in the night,
Fearing the dawn, escaping the light.
In whispered thoughts, I want to say,
In shadows deep, forever stay.

Fragments of Silent Whispers

In the hush of twilight's grace,
Soft secrets linger in the air,
Every shadow wears your trace,
A fleeting dance, both light and rare.

Echoes wander through the night,
Where forgotten hopes softly sigh,
Lost in a realm of silver light,
Dreams awaken, time drifts by.

Whispers carry, softly weave,
Threads of stories, faint and fine,
In this silence, hearts believe,
Fragments of love, a rare design.

Beneath the stars, our spirits blend,
In each moment, we confide,
These silent whispers never end,
Eternity, our gentle guide.

Pieces of a Dreaming Mind

In the maze of twilight's hue,
Thoughts like stars begin to play,
Colorful shards in shades anew,
Crafting worlds where secrets lay.

Fragments swirl in endless skies,
Where wishes drift on whispered streams,
Every heartbeat softly ties,
Reality to fragile dreams.

With each thought, a tapestry,
Woven fine with silver threads,
Echoes of what's meant to be,
In this space, the soul now treads.

Lost in visions, drifting high,
Pieces dance, a vivid sign,
In the quiet, hear the cry,
Of a mind, so pure, divine.

Hearts Entwined in Enigma

In the shadows where we meet,
Mysteries weave their gentle spell,
Silent glances, a heartbeat's beat,
A secret only time can tell.

Two souls cast in twilight's glow,
Bound by threads both soft and tight,
A labyrinth where feelings flow,
Each embrace ignites the night.

Words unspoken hold our fate,
In every pause, a tale unfolds,
Entwined lives, we learn to wait,
In the silence, love beholds.

Ah, the dance of fate's design,
In enigma, our hearts find home,
Together, we write the divine,
Two as one, through realms we roam.

Riddles of the Unspoken Soul

In the depths where silence breathes,
Questions linger on the edge,
Like a storm that gently seethes,
Here we stand, a whispered pledge.

Hidden truths beneath our skin,
In each sigh, a world unfolds,
Riddles wrapped in softest din,
Secrets treasured, yet untold.

Eyes that speak when words fall short,
A glance kindles what's unseen,
In this dance, we find the port,
Where unspoken dreams convene.

Through the shadows, lanterns glide,
Guiding hearts that yearn to know,
In this place, we cannot hide,
The unspoken truth will flow.

Milton Keynes UK
Ingram Content Group UK Ltd.
UKHW021938121124
451129UK00007B/137